Ready for Your First Period?

The Complete Girls' Guide to Puberty & Period Basics.

AGES 9–12

Serena Lark

Checklliste how-to

FEEL READY— NOT WORRIED

All Rights Reserved.
Copyright @ 2025 Serena Lark
No part of this publication may be reproduced, stored in a retrieval system, or transmitted in any form or by any means—electronic, mechanical, photocopying, recording, or otherwise—without the prior written permission of the publisher.

The information contained in this book is provided for informational purposes only. While every effort has been made to ensure accuracy, neither the author nor the publisher makes any warranties, express or implied, with respect to the completeness or effectiveness of the material. The author and publisher shall not be held liable for any damages, losses, or injuries arising directly or indirectly from the use or misuse of the information, advice, or techniques described herein.

A Special Bonus Just for You!

Because you picked up this book, I created something extra just for you:

✅ **Color Your Power – 50 affirmation prompts** + coloring pages to help you stay calm and confident

✅ **Snack & Sip Fun Book – 10 no-cook recipes** you can make all by yourself

✅ **My 12-Month First Period Planner** – a year-long tracker for your cycle, feelings, energy, and wins

🎁 *Exclusive Extras (Only in This Book)*

👉 Please turn to page **41** and scan the QR code to access all this free material I've prepared especially for you.

Thank you again—and enjoy!

Index

Introduction.   7

  A Special Letter Just for You – From Your Big Sister.   7
  What This Book Is and How It Will Help..   9
  A Quick Note for Parents or Guardians.   10

Part 1 – Understanding Your Amazing Body.   11

  1.1 What It Means to Grow Up..   12
  1.2 All Those Changes – Inside and Out.   15
  1.3 Breasts, Hair, Smells... Totally Normal!.   18
  1.4 Your Period, Explained..   20
  1.5 What Is a Period?.   23
  1.6 When Does It Come? How Long Does It Last?.   26

Part 2 – Getting Ready for Your First Period.   30

  2.1 Signs It Might Be Coming Soon..   31
  2.2 The Ultimate Period Survival Kit.   33
  2.3 DIY: Decorate Your Kit! (Fun Activity).   36
  2.4 Talking About It with People You Trust.   38
  2.5 How to Tell Mom, Dad, Teachers, or Friends.   39

Part 3 – Your Period Has Arrived!   45

  3.1 What to Do When It Starts – Step by Step..   46
  3.2 Pads, Tampons, Cups – What's Right for You?.   48
  3.3 Simple Guide + Pros and Cons Chart.   50
  3.4 Staying Clean and Comfy.   55

    3.5 Cramps, Cravings & Weird Feelings.   57
    3.6 Natural Remedies to Feel Better.   62

Part 4 – Feelings, Confidence & Being You.   66

    4.1 Mood Swings and "Off" Days.   67
    4.2 Feeling Shy or Embarrassed? You're Not Alone.   69
    4.3 What to Say If Someone Makes a Joke.   72
    4.4 Body Confidence & Self-Love.   74
    4.5 Positive Affirmations + Confidence Boosters.   76

Part 5 – Real Talk & Pro Tips.   80

    5.1 Things No One Tells You (But Should).   81
    5.2 Periods at School, on Trips, During Sports.   83
    5.3 No Pad? No Problem!.   86
    5.4 What to Do in a Period Emergency.   87
    5.5 Myths to Bust.   89
    5.6 Real Questions from Real Girls (Q&A Style).   93

Appendix: When to Ask for Help   99

Appendix for Parents.   110

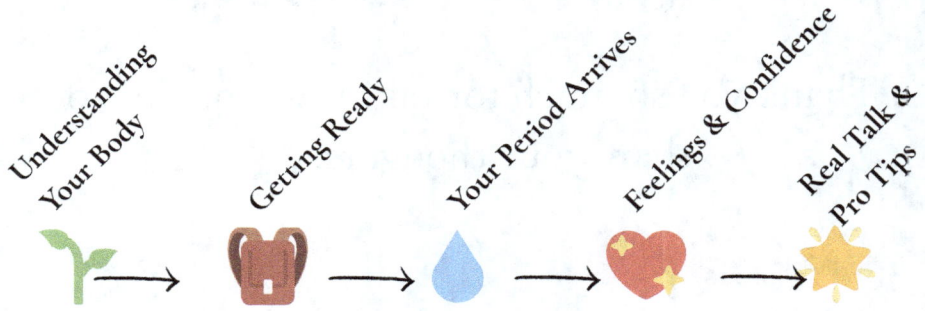

Your Feedback Means the World!

I truly appreciate your feedback.

Thank you so much for taking a moment to share your thoughts! 🙏

INTRODUCTION

A Special Letter Just for You From Your Big Sister Sophie

Hey sweet girl,

I'm Sophie — your big sister for this book — and I'm so glad you're here with me. The fact that you're holding this guide means you're curious, brave, and ready to figure out something really important about yourself.

I still remember when I first started hearing whispers about "getting your period." Honestly? I felt nervous and a little clueless. But then I realized every girl goes through it — and once you know what's happening, it's not so scary.

With the right info, a few tips, and some confidence boosters, you'll be ready for this next chapter of growing up.

Growing up can feel weird sometimes — surprising, exciting, and yes, even a little awkward. But all of it is normal. Your body is doing something incredible: changing, growing stronger, and becoming more you.

And I'm here to help you understand it, feel proud of it, and even have a little fun along the way.

In these pages, I'll share answers to the questions I once had, tricks to make tough days easier, and activities I wish I'd known about back then — from decorating a period kit to making the best comfort snacks when cravings hit.

So take a deep breath. You've got this. And I've got your back — every step of the way.

💖 Sophie.

What This Book Is and How It Will Help

This isn't just a book about periods — it's your friendly guide to growing up with confidence, care, and a little fun.
We'll talk about what's happening to your body, feelings, and life as you step into this new stage.

Inside, you'll learn what's really going on during your first period, how to prepare, what to do when it starts, and how to handle cramps, mood swings, cravings. Most importantly, you'll discover how to feel proud, strong, and totally you through it all.

You'll also find checklists, activities, journal pages, snack ideas, and secret tips no one talks about. This book is your safe space!.
Wherever you are in your journey, you're already doing great. Let's dive in!

A Quick Note for Parents or Guardians

Dear Parent or Guardian,
Thank you for choosing this book to guide your child through puberty. Written for girls ages 9–12 in a warm, big-sister style, it aims to make the first period and related changes clear, positive, and manageable.

Inside are simple explanations, confidence-boosting tips, and bonus tools like a period tracker, affirmations, snack ideas, plus a short appendix with guidance for you.
We hope it inspires open, reassuring conversations and helps your child feel confident and proud on this journey.

With warmth,
The Author

PART 1
UNDERSTANDING YOUR AMAZING BODY

1.1
What It Means to Grow Up

Hey, it's Sophie again.
This book was made just for girls like you — curious, growing, and ready to understand all the changes happening in your body (and heart, and mind too!).

You might be feeling a little nervous, a little excited, or a little "I-don't-know-how-to-feel-about-this" — and that's totally okay. Growing up doesn't come with a rulebook, but this guide is here to help you figure things out — like a big sister would.

Inside, you'll find answers to your questions, tips to feel confident about your body, and fun extras like a period tracker, inspiring affirmations, and even snack ideas for those "craving days."

We'll talk about puberty, your first period, and everything that comes with becoming your amazing, strong, one-of-a-kind self.

No shame. No weird stuff. Just real talk — because you deserve to feel informed, confident, and proud of who you're becoming.

Let's figure it all out, together.
You've got this — and I've got your back.

YOU'RE GROWING CHECKLIST

Check off anything that feels true for you (and it's totally okay if not all of them do — yet!)

- ○ I've noticed some changes in my body
- ○ I feel more emotional than I used to
- ○ I like learning how to take care of myself
- ○ I'm starting to see myself a little differently
- ○ I want to understand it what's happening
- ○ I've started caring about privacy or "me time"
- ○ I feel a little different around friends sometimes
- ○ I began to notice things about emotions/moods

1.2
All Those Changes Inside and Out

Growing up doesn't happen all at once — it's more like a bunch of little changes that show up one by one, like surprise guests at a party. Some changes are easy to notice, and others happen quietly inside your body.

You might...
- feel more emotional some days — like laughing one minute and crying the next
- start to see new hair growing under your arms or around your private parts
- notice your breasts beginning to develop
- sweat more than before (yes, even if it's not hot!)
- see changes in your skin, like getting oilier or a few pimples
- have different thoughts, stronger opinions, or even crushes (!)

And guess what? All of that is totally normal.
These changes are part of something called puberty — a fancy word for the time when your body gets ready to become more grown-up. It doesn't mean you're not still a kid in many ways — it just means your body is growing and shifting, and that's a good thing!

Some changes might feel exciting — like getting taller or wearing your first real bra. Others might feel awkward or even a little embarrassing — like body odor or mood swings. But none of it means there's anything wrong with you. These changes happen to everyone, just not always at the same time or in the same way.

You're unique, and your journey will look a little different from your friends'. That's what makes growing up so special — it's yours.

Spot the Change!

Circle, color, or check the ones you've already noticed — and don't worry if you haven't seen some of them yet. Everyone develops on their own schedule!

- ○ I've grown taller
- ○ I've started getting some pimples
- ○ I sweat more than I used to
- ○ I've noticed some body hair growing
- ○ My moods change quickly sometimes
- ○ My chest is starting to change
- ○ I feel more curious about crushes or feelings
- ○ I've had questions about what's happening

Did you know

Puberty usually starts between ages 8 and 13 — but everyone's timing is different.
So if your changes feel early or late... they're still just right for you.

1.3
Breasts, Hair, Smells? Totally Normal

Growing up doesn't happen all at once — it's more like a bunch of little changes that show up one by one, like surprise guests at a party. Some changes are easy to notice, and others happen quietly inside your body.

Breasts

You might notice tiny bumps under your nipples — kind of like little soft buttons. That's your breast tissue starting to grow. For some girls, one side grows faster than the other (totally normal!). They might feel sore or tender sometimes — like a bruise — especially if they get bumped.

You might start thinking about wearing a training bra. Don't worry — there's no "right time." If you want one for comfort, support, or confidence, that's your choice. You do you.

Body Hair

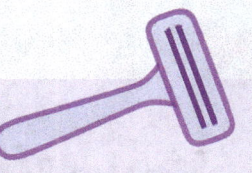

Hair might show up in new places: under your arms, around your private parts, even on your legs or upper lip. It might feel like, "Whoa, where did that come from?!" But body hair is just another sign your body is growing up.

Some girls start shaving, others don't. That's a personal decision — and you can talk to someone you trust (like a parent or guardian) about it if you're unsure.

Body Smells

Let's talk sweat and body odor. As your sweat glands start working differently, you might notice... um, smells. Especially after P.E. or on hot days.

This doesn't mean you're dirty — it just means it's time to start using deodorant or washing more carefully under your arms. Clean habits = fresh confidence.

And hey — everyone goes through it.
No one smells like roses 24/7.

1.4
Your Period, Explained

You've probably heard the word "period" before, maybe in health class or whispered between friends.

<u>But what is it, really?</u>

It's something your body will start doing once it's ready, like a message "Your body is growing up!"

It's part of something called the menstrual cycle, which is your body's natural rhythm that prepares it for a possible pregnancy someday (in the future!).

But for now, all you need to know is this:

- About once a month, a small amount of blood comes out of your vagina.
- It usually lasts about 3–7 days.
- It happens to all girls and women — it's a totally normal, healthy part of growing up.

Your period doesn't mean something's wrong. It means your body is working just as it should.

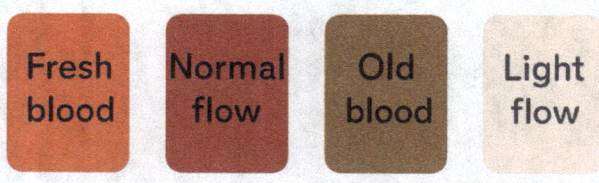

What Does It Look Like?

The blood from your period doesn't gush out like in the movies — it's more like a slow flow. It might be bright red, brownish, or pinkish. Every girl's period looks a little different, and that's totally okay.

Will I Know When It's Coming?

Sometimes, yes! You might feel a little crampy, moody, or notice discharge (that's a clear or white fluid in your underwear) a few months before your first period shows up. We'll talk more about those signs in the next part of the book.

The most important thing to remember? Your period is not gross. It's not weird. It's natural, and it means your body is amazing.

Almost half the people in the world get periods.

You're part of something big, brave, and beautiful.

Sophie's Story #1
The First Surprise

"OMG, I'll never forget the first time I saw a red spot on my underwear. My heart started racing and I felt like everyone around me could tell. I wanted to cry and hide at the same time. But then I remembered what my mom had told me—'just breathe and go to the bathroom.' I did, and guess what? It wasn't nearly as scary once I took that first step."

Lesson:
Sometimes the scariest moment is just the first one. You're braver than you think!

1.5
What Is a Period?

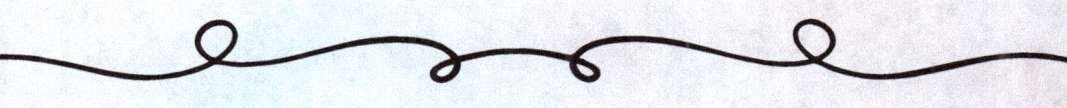

Okay, let's zoom in a little deeper — because I promise, once you understand what's happening, it feels way less confusing.

Here's how I like to think about it: each month, your body gets ready just in case you might grow a baby someday (way, waaay in the future — not now!). To prepare, your uterus — that's a small, pear-shaped muscle low in your belly — builds up a soft, squishy lining. Think of it like a cozy, fluffy blanket.

Now, if your body doesn't need that blanket (which it won't for many years), it lets it go. And that "letting go" is what we call your period.

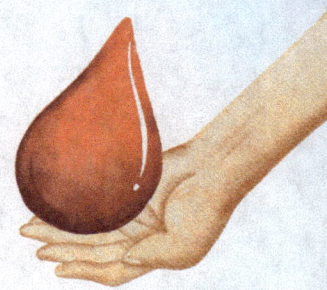

So, a period is simply your body releasing that extra lining. It comes out of your vagina in the form of blood — sometimes light, sometimes a little heavier — and it usually lasts a few days.

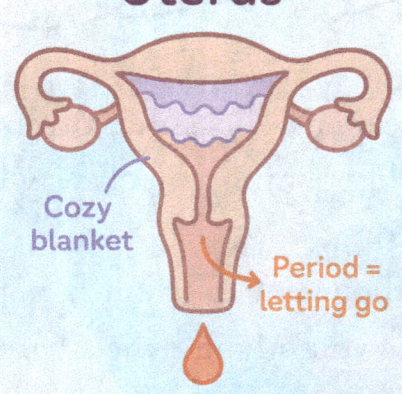

That's it! Not scary. Not dirty. Not something to be ashamed of. Just your body doing what it was designed to do.

When I finally understood this, I went from feeling nervous to thinking, "Oh... that's all it is?" And honestly, it felt kind of empowering. My body wasn't betraying me — it was working perfectly.

Try this!

Design your own "My Period Symbol" — something that represents how you want to feel about your period.

Maybe it's a moon (for its monthly rhythm), a flower (for blooming and growing), or even a superhero symbol (because you're powerful!). What would your symbol look like?

1.6
When Does It Come? How Long Does It Last?

When Will I Get my Period?

"Here's the honest answer: It's different for everyone. Most girls get their first period between the ages of 9 and 14, but some start a little earlier or later — and that's perfectly okay.

Your body has its own perfect timing. You might already notice signs it's on the way (we'll cover those in Part 2), or it might surprise you one day. Either way, you'll be ready!

How Long Does A Period Last?

Most periods last about 3 to 7 days.

The flow might be light at first, get heavier in the middle, then get lighter again. Some girls only need a few pads or liners per day, others more — both are normal.

And once you get your first period, it usually comes back about once a month. That's called your cycle, and it can be anywhere from 21 to 35 days long. It might take a while to become regular — especially in the first year or two.

Question	Quick Answer
When might it start?	Ages 9–14 (sometimes earlier or later)
How long does it last?	About 3–7 days
How often does it come?	Every 21–35 days (average: 28)
Is it the same for everyone?	Nope! Everyone's cycle is unique

Totally Normal Facts

- Some girls get their period before their friends — others after. Both are normal.
- Your first few periods might be irregular — that's normal too.
- You might have some cramps or no cramps at all. Both are okay.
- If you're a late bloomer, there's nothing wrong with you. Pinky promise.

TRUE OR FALSE?

Puberty Happens Overnight

QUESTION:

Puberty is something that happens all at once, like waking up one morning completely changed.

True or False?

→ Answer at the bottom!

Sophie Says: Your body is amazing — periods are just one of the ways it shows how well it works.

Answer: ✗ False! Puberty is a gradual process that happens over several years. Some changes show up earlier, others later — and that's totally normal.

QUICK CHECK

What Really Happens During a Period?

CIRCLE THE ANSWERS THAT ARE TRUE:

1. A period means your body is releasing blood and tissue it doesn't need.
2. It's your body's way of saying it's healthy and growing.
3. Period blood gushes out like in the movies.
4. Every girl's flow looks a little different — and that's normal.

✓ 1, 2, and 4 are true.
✗ 3 is false — periods are usually a slow flow, not a dramatic gush.

PART 2
GETTING READY FOR YOUR FIRST PERIOD

2.1
Signs It Might Be Coming Soon

I'll never forget the first little hints my body gave me that my period was on the way. For me, it started with my breasts feeling sore, like tiny bruises. Then one day, I noticed a bit of white discharge in my underwear and thought, "Wait... what is this?" At first I was embarrassed, but later I realized — it was just my body's way of saying, "Get ready, Sophie, things are changing."

BODY CLUES CHECKLIST

Check off any signs you've noticed.
And remember — it's okay if you haven't seen all of them yet.

- ○ My breasts are starting to grow or feel sore
- ○ I've noticed clear discharge in my underwear
- ○ I sometimes feel extra moody or emotional
- ○ I'm getting a little bit of acne or oily skin
- ○ Hair grows under my arms/in my private parts
- ○ I've had some cramping or strange belly feelings
- ○ I'm growing faster or my clothes fit differently
- ○ I'm more aware of my body or privacy

HAVE YOU NOTICED?

Take a few minutes to think about what your body is telling you. You can jot down a few thoughts here — there's no wrong way to do it!

Some changes I've noticed in myself:

And here's something I wish someone had told me: noticing these signs doesn't mean your period will start tomorrow. It could still be weeks or months away. But it does mean your body is on its own amazing timeline, one step at a time.

You're not behind.

You're not too early.

 You're exactly where you need to be. 💖

— Sophie

2.2
The Ultimate Period Survival Kit

Imagine this: your period starts at school, at a sleepover, or right before dance class. Are you ready? You will be — with your very own Period Survival Kit!

This little kit is like a secret sidekick. You can keep it in your backpack, locker, or bedside drawer, and it'll have everything you need just in case.

Let's build it together!

Build Your Kit!

Here's a checklist of things you might want to include. Some are must-haves, some are nice extras, and some are just for you.

ESSENTIALS
- ⭕ Pads (at least 2–3)
- ⭕ A clean pair of underwear
- ⭕ Wipes or tissues
- ⭕ Small zip pouch or makeup bag
- ⭕ Hand sanitizer

NICE EXTRAS
- ⭕ A tiny snack (chocolate? trail mix? yum!)
- ⭕ Travel-size deodorant
- ⭕ Pain relief (ask an adult before adding this!)
- ⭕ A heating patch (great for cramps)

PERSONAL TOUCHES
- ⭕ A mini notepad or journal
- ⭕ A small mirror
- ⭕ A positive note to yourself (seriously!)
- ⭕ Stickers or decorations that make you smile

Sophie's Story #2
The Missing Pad

"One day at school, my period started early and I didn't have my kit with me. Panic mode, right? I used toilet paper to hold me over and asked a friend if she had a spare pad. She smiled and handed me one like it was no big deal. That tiny act of kindness taught me: girls have each other's backs."

Lesson:
You're never alone. Asking for help is strong, not weak.

2.3
DIY: Decorate Your Kit!

Your period kit or pouch isn't just a bunch of supplies — it's yours. And when something is personal, it feels more special, less scary, and even kinda fun.
So why not decorate it like the awesome, powerful thing it is?
Time to Get Creative! Grab some stickers, markers, washi tape, fabric pens — anything you like.
Make your pouch or bag look like YOU.
One day you'll thank yourself for being so prepared.
— Sophie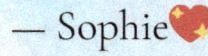

Here are some fun ideas to try:

- Add your name or a fun nickname
- Draw cute doodles like hearts, flowers, or stars
- Use patches, pins, or charms for decoration
- Write a little phrase on it like:

Design Zone!
Use this space to sketch out your pouch design before decorating the real thing:

" My Power Pouch"

" Be Brave, Be You"

" I've Got This"

" Period? No Big Deal."

2.4
Talking About It with People You Trust

You don't have to go through this alone. It's totally okay — and actually super smart — to talk about your body and your period with someone you trust. Whether you have questions, worries, or just want to say, "Hey... I think it's starting," the right person will be there for you.

Not everyone is easy to talk to — and that's okay too.

The key is to find someone who listens, cares, and won't judge you. Even just starting with one small question can open up a great conversation.

People You Might Trust
A parent or guardian
An older sister or cousin
A favorite aunt
A teacher or school nurse
A friend who gets it

2.5
How to Tell Mom, Dad, Teachers, Friends

Telling someone you trust that your period has started (or might start soon) can feel a little awkward at first — but it doesn't have to be scary.

In fact, the people who care about you will want to help! They might not always know what to say right away, but starting the conversation is a brave first step — and once you do it, you'll feel so much better. Let's make it easier together.

What Would You Say?
You're at school and realize your period just started. I would say:
_____
You want to tell your dad but don't know how to start. I would say:
_____
A friend jokes about periods and you feel embarrassed. I would say:
_____

You are stronger, smarter, and braver than you think.
Starting a conversation takes courage — but you've got this.

Practice Scripts

Here are a few ways you can say it. Try them out loud or in your head. Then change the words to sound like you.

To a parent or guardian:

"Hey Mom, I think my period might be starting soon."
"I'm having some changes... can we talk about it?"
"Can you help me make a period kit, just in case?"

To a teacher or school nurse:

"Hi, I think I started my period and I don't have any supplies."
"Can I go to the nurse? I'm not feeling well."
"I need to use the bathroom — it's kind of urgent."

To a friend:

"Have you had your period yet? I think mine might be coming."
"Do you have an extra pad? I forgot mine."
"Wanna help me make a kit for school?"

Your Feedback Means the World!

I truly appreciate your feedback.

Thank you so much for taking a moment to share your thoughts! 🙏

A Special Bonus Just for You!

Because you picked up this book, I created something extra just for you:

✅ <u>**Color Your Power – 50 affirmation prompts**</u> + coloring pages to help you stay calm and confident

✅ <u>**Snack & Sip Fun Book – 10 no-cook recipes**</u> you can make all by yourself

✅ <u>**My 12-Month First Period Planner**</u> – a year-long tracker for your cycle, feelings, energy, and wins

👉 Scan the QR code to access all this free material I've prepared especially for you.

🎁 Exclusive Extras (Only in This Book)

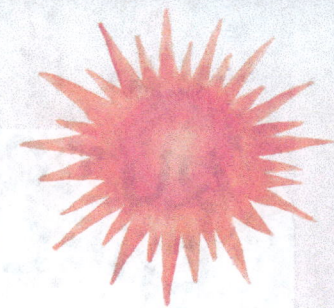

Only Pads Work for Your First Period
QUESTION:

When you get your first period, the only product you can use is a pad.

True or False?

→ Answer at the bottom!

Sophie Says: Your body is amYour body, your choice — there's no "one right way" to manage your period.

Answer: ✖ False!
Pads are a great choice for beginners, but they're not the only option. Some girls prefer liners, period underwear, or even tampons later on. What matters most is choosing what feels safe and comfortable for you.

QUICK CHECK

What Belongs in a Period Kit?

Circle the things that belong in a "PERIOD SURVIVAL KIT":

1. Pads or liners
2. Extra underwear
3. Hand sanitizer
4. A slice of pizza
5. Wipes or tissues
6. A tiny snack
7. A small pouch or bag.

→ Answer at the bottom!

✓ 1, 2, 3, 5, 6, and 7 all belong.
✗ 4 (pizza!) is just for fun — snacks are great, but maybe not in your pouch.

PART 3
YOUR PERIOD HAS ARRIVED!

3.1
What to Do When It Starts

I'll never forget the day it finally happened to me. I looked down and saw a little blood in my underwear, and my brain went straight to panic mode. *"What do I do now?"* I whispered to myself.

It's okay. You're okay. This is the moment your body has been gently preparing for — and guess what? You're so ready.

Let's walk through it together, step by step — the same way I did when I asked myself, *"Sophie, what's the very first thing you should do?"*

Don't panic.
It might feel surprising, exciting, weird, or even scary — all of those feelings are normal.

Go to the bathroom.
Find a private place where you feel safe. If you're at school, ask to go to the nurse or restroom.

3 Clean up gently.
Use toilet paper or wipes to clean the area. If you have a pad or liner, now's the time to use it!

4 Change your underwear if needed.
If you packed an extra pair, awesome! If not, ask a trusted adult (they will understand).

5 Tell someone you trust.
You don't have to go through it alone. Even just saying, "I think I started my period" is enough.

6 Give yourself a mental high-five.
You're growing. You're learning. You're doing amazing.

Stay calm   Bathroom   Clean up   Change underwear   Tell someone

3.2
Pads, Tampons, Cups

Now that your period has arrived, you'll need something to catch the flow and keep you feeling clean, dry, and confident. But which product is right for you?

Let's break it down.

There are three main options:
- Pads (also called sanitary pads or liners)
- Tampons
- Menstrual cups

Each one works in a different way, and each has its own pros and cons. The most important thing? You get to choose what you're most comfortable with — and that might change over time.

PADS

Pads stick to your underwear and catch blood outside your body. They come in all shapes and sizes: some are thin and light, others are longer for more coverage.

-Easy to use
-Great for first-timers
-No need to insert anything
-Can feel bulky if not placed right
-Needs changing every few hours

TAMPONS

Tampons go inside your body to absorb blood before it leaves. They're small, often with an applicator, and some girls use them when swimming.

-Discreet and great for active days
-You can swim and do sports
-Can feel tricky to insert at first
-Need to be changed every 4–8 hours
-Not everyone feels ready right away (and that's okay!)

CUPS

These are soft, reusable silicone cups that you insert into your vagina to collect blood. They last for years and are eco-friendly.

-You can wear them up to 12 hours
-Better for the environment
-Need to be cleaned and inserted properly
-Not usually used by first-timers (but still an option later!)

I think I want to try: _____

3.3
Simple Guide + Pros and Cons Chart

How to Use a Pad (Step-by-Step)

1. Take the pad out of its wrapper.
2. Peel off the sticky backing.
3. Stick the pad onto the inside of your underwear, right in the middle.
4. If it has wings, fold them around your underwear.
5. Change it every 3–5 hours, or when it feels wet or full.
6. Throw the used pad in the trash, never the toilet!

Tip: Always keep a couple of extra pads in your pouch — just in case.

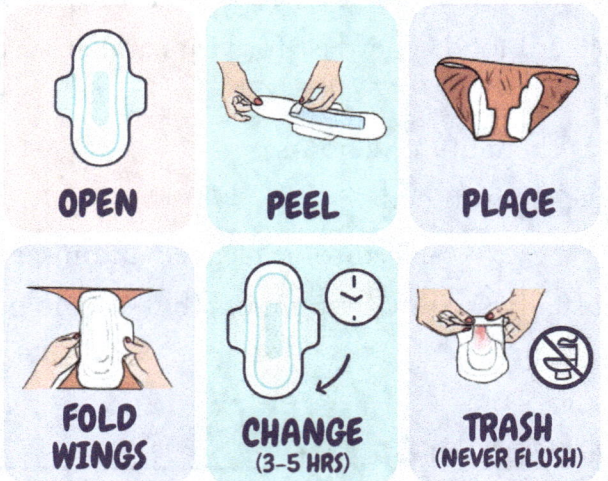

How to Use a Tampon (With Applicator)

1. Wash your hands.
2. Hold the tampon at the grip (middle) with one hand.
3. Sit or stand in a comfy position (some girls try squatting or putting one foot up).
4. Gently guide the tip into your vagina and push the inner part of the applicator in.
5. Pull the plastic part out — the string stays outside.
6. Change every 4–8 hours. To remove: gently pull the string.

Tip: Try it at home first with the help of an adult, and don't stress — it might take a few tries!

How to Use a Menstrual Cup (Quick Intro)

1. Wash your hands.
2. Fold the cup into a "C" shape.
3. Gently insert it into your vagina (aim it back, not up).
4. Let it open and sit comfortably — it will catch your flow.
5. After 6–8 hours, remove it by pinching the base and pulling it out slowly.
6. Rinse and reinsert — or store in its pouch if you're done for the day.

Tip: Cups are usually better for later on — once you're more used to your body and your flow.

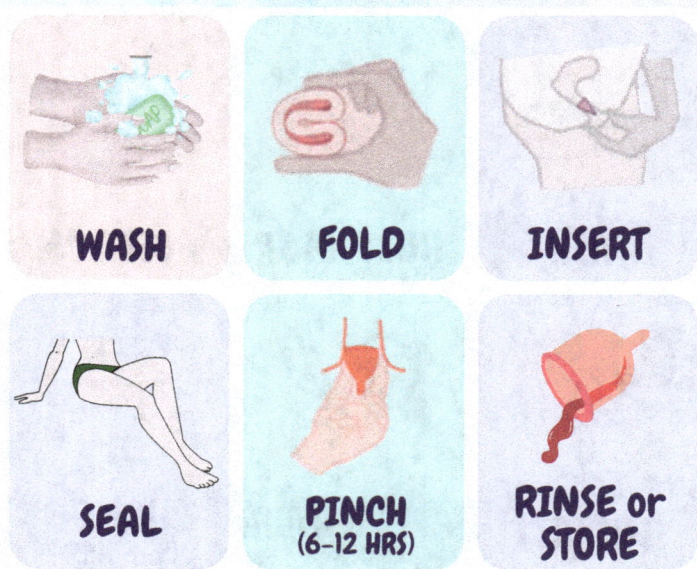

Using Tampons

You might have heard about something called **TSS (Toxic Shock Syndrome)**. The name sounds super scary — I remember feeling nervous the first time I read about it! But here's the truth: TSS is **very rare,** and tampons are safe when you use them the right way.

Here's what to keep in mind:
- Change your tampon every 4–8 hours (never longer).
- Always choose the lowest absorbency that works for your flow.
- If you ever feel really sick — like fever, dizziness, vomiting, or a strange rash — tell an adult right away.

And here's the best part: you have options! **Pads are perfect for beginners** and just as safe. Later on, if you decide to try tampons, you'll already know the smart way to use them.

💖 *Millions of girls and women use tampons safely every single day. The key is simple: change them on time and listen to your body.*
— Sophie

Using a Menstrual Cup

Menstrual cups might sound new or even a little weird at first — I remember thinking, *"How does that even work?"* But lots of women and some older teens use them safely. They're reusable, eco-friendly, and can hold more flow than a pad or tampon.

Here's what you need to know to use them safely:
- Wash your hands before and after inserting or removing the cup.
- Empty and rinse the cup at least every 8–12 hours (never longer).
- Clean it well between cycles — follow the instructions that come with the cup.
- If you ever feel pain, irritation, or can't remove it, stop and ask an adult for help.

💖 *Cups can be a great option later on, when you feel ready. There's no rush — pads are usually the easiest place to start. The important thing is choosing what makes you feel comfortable and confident.*
— Sophie

3.4
Staying Clean and Comfy

Having your period doesn't mean you have to feel gross, uncomfortable, or stressed.
With just a few habits and smart tricks, you can stay fresh, clean, and confident no matter where you are!

Hygiene Tips

Keeping your body clean helps you feel better and stay healthy. Here's how:

- Wash your private area once or twice a day with warm water. You don't need fancy soaps!
- Always wipe front to back after using the bathroom.
- Change your pad or tampon every 3–5 hours — or sooner if it feels full.
- Don't forget to change your underwear daily (and keep an extra pair in your bag!).

Tip: If you're not at home, moist wipes or a little pack of tissues can be lifesavers.

Outfit Hacks

Some days you'll want to dress cozy — and some days you'll want to feel stylish. You can do both!

- Choose dark-colored bottoms (like black leggings or navy shorts) just in case of leaks.
- Keep a sweater or sweatshirt in your bag — it's great for warmth and coverage.
- Use long shirts/layer to help you feel more secure.
- Period underwear? Total game changer. (Ask a parent if you're curious!)

Tip: Leak-proof period panties are comfy, washable, and can be worn with or without a pad.

Bathroom Basics (a.k.a. Real-Life Hacks)

- Carry your pouch with confidence — nobody is watching as closely as you think.
- If you need help at school, go to the nurse or quietly ask a trusted teacher.

Always throw pads and tampons in the trash — not the toilet!

3.5
Cramps, Cravings & Weird Feelings

Periods aren't just about pads and tampons — they can bring all sorts of feelings too.
Some are physical (like cramps), and others are emotional (like mood swings).

Sometimes you just want to curl up with a blanket, a snack, and your favorite playlist — and you know what? That's totally okay.

Let's talk about what's going on — and how to feel better.

Remember: feelings aren't facts. They come and go — and you're strong enough to ride the wave.

Some girls feel a dull ache in their lower belly or back before/during their period. These are cramps, and they happen because your uterus is squeezing a little to let go of the blood.

Cramps

Ways to ease cramps:
- Use a warm heating pad or hot water bottle on your tummy
- Try light stretching or yoga
- Drink water — yes, it actually helps!
- Rest if you're tired
- If it really hurts, talk to a parent about taking pain relief

Ever feel like you need chocolate? Or something salty, sweet? That's a craving and super common during your period. Your body's hormone changes can make you hungrier or picky about what you want to eat.

Smart snack ideas:

Cravings

- Dark chocolate (just a square or two!)
- Peanut butter + banana
- Fresh fruit with yogurt
- Cheese and whole grain crackers
- Popcorn or pretzels (with water to stay balanced)

Tip: Try to eat small meals throughout the day and don't skip breakfast — it helps stabilize your mood and energy.

Some days you might feel emotional, sensitive, annoyed, or just not yourself. That's normal.: hormones can play games with your mood, but you're still you.

Mini Mood Boosters

Mood Swings

- Write a note to yourself: "This will pass."
- Text a friend who gets you
- Go outside and breathe some fresh air
- Dance to your favorite song
- Hug your pet (or a pillow!)

Cat-Cow

Child's Pose

Gentle Twist

Feelings Journal
Use this space to check in with yourself. Write down what you're feeling — no judgment, just honesty.

Today I'm feeling...

Sophie's Story #3
The Cramp Attack

"I was at soccer practice when cramps hit me out of nowhere. I doubled over, thinking something was seriously wrong. Coach let me sit out, and I used a heating pad later at home. I realized it was just my uterus doing its thing, not some emergency. The pain passed, and I felt proud for handling it."

Lesson:
Cramps can be tough, but they don't mean something is broken. You can manage them.

3.6
Natural Remedies to Feel Better

Sometimes your body just needs a little extra love during your period.
Luckily, there are simple, natural things you can do to feel better — no harsh medicine required (unless you need it, of course!).
Let's build your personal feel-better toolkit.

1 **Warmth is your bestie:** Place a warm heating pad or hot water bottle on your lower belly. It helps relax your muscles and melt away the cramps.

2 **Stretch it out:** Even light movement can boost blood flow and ease the tension.

3 **Drink** something coz Herbal teas can help you relax and soothe your stomach. Feel-Good Sips: Peppermint tea, Chamomile tea, Ginger tea.

♡ **Bonus**: Wrap your hands around a warm mug and breathe in the steam — instant calm.

Comfort Corner

Here are more calming things you can try:
Take a warm bath with bubbles or bath salts
Cuddle up with a fuzzy blanket and your favorite book or movie
Journal your thoughts, color something cozy
Light a candle or use a diffuser with lavender
Listen to slow music/soft podcast while lying down

TRY THIS FIRST!

Instead of reaching for medicine right away, try this mini routine:

○ Warm pad
○ Gentle stretches
○ Herbal tea
○ Deep breaths
○ Cozy socks
○ Positive words: "I'm okay. This will pass."

**Taking care of yourself is not a weakness — it's a superpower.
And the more you learn to listen to your body…
the more you'll know exactly how to treat it with kindness.**

TRUE OR FALSE?

You Can't Swim on Your Period

QUESTION:

When you're on your period, you can't go swimming.

True or False?

→ Answer at the bottom!

Sophie Says: Your period shouldn't stop you from doing what you love — even swimming!

Answer: ✗ False! With the right product — like a tampon or period swimwear — you can swim safely and comfortably. Pads don't work well in water, but that doesn't mean swimming is off-limits.

QUICK CHECK

Cramp Fixes — Which Ones Help?

CIRCLE THE THINGS THAT REALLY HELP WITH CRAMPS:

1. A warm heating pad or hot water bottle
2. Gentle exercise like stretching or walking
3. Eating salty chips and soda all day
4. Rest and deep breathing
5. Staying hydrated (water, tea)

→ Answer at the bottom!

✅ 1, 2, 4, and 5 can all help ease cramps.
❌ 3 might taste good, but it won't make cramps better (and might make you feel worse).

PART 4
FEELINGS, CONFIDENCE & BEING YOU

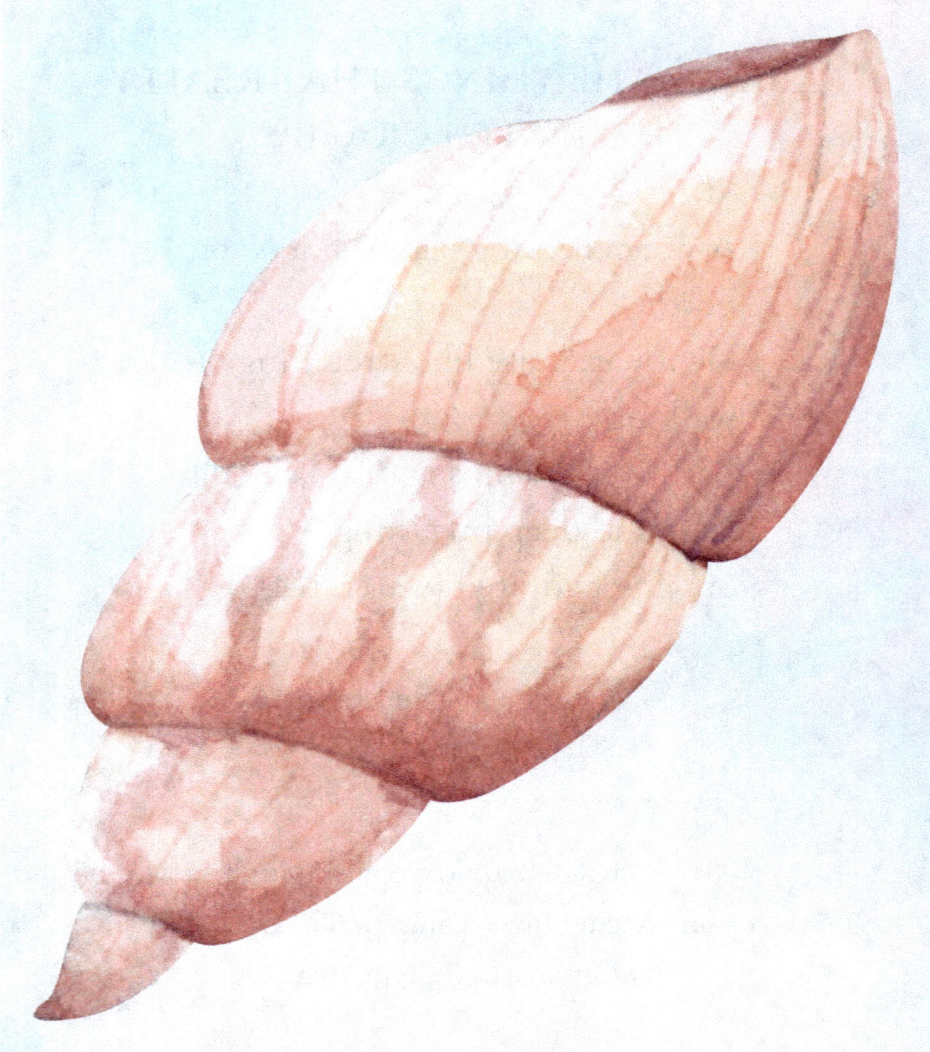

4.1
Mood Swings and "Off" Days

Some days, everything feels off.
You might wake up feeling fine...
then snap at your little
brother, cry over a
commercial, and want
to hide under your
blanket — all before lunch.
Sound familiar?
If so, welcome to the world
of mood swings — and guess what?
You're not alone.

What's Going On?

When your body starts going through puberty, your hormones are doing their thing behind the scenes. And sometimes, they make your emotions feel like they're on a rollercoaster.
That doesn't mean you're being dramatic.
It means your body and brain are figuring things out.
And it's okay.

Let's check in. How are you feeling right now?
Circle or color as many as you want — feelings can change during the day!

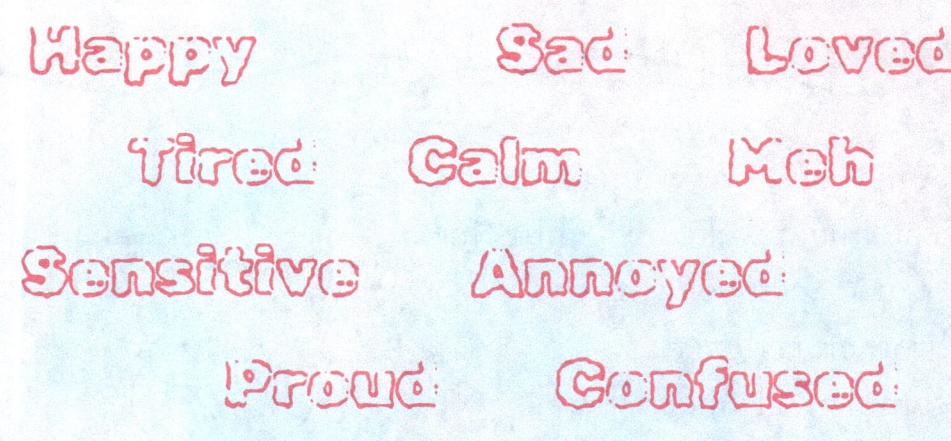

Take it from me, Sophie: even on the wildest "off" days, your feelings are real — and they will pass.

Need ideas? Try deep breaths, stretching, listening to music, journaling, talking to someone, or just sitting quietly with a cozy blanket.

Your feelings are real — even if they're messy or don't make sense.

What matters is being kind to yourself and remembering: this will pass.

4.2
Feeling Shy or Embarrassed?

Let's be honest:
Sometimes just thinking about your period, your body, or even saying the word "menstruation" out loud can make you want to disappear into the floor.
That's okay. That's normal.
Growing up comes with all kinds of new stuff — and not all of it feels comfy right away.

Why We Feel Embarrassed

- You're going through things others not see
- You don't know what's "normal" yet
- You feel like everyone is looking (they're not!)
- You don't want to say the wrong thing
- You're learning to be okay with change

Every single girl has felt awkward
or shy at some point. Yes, even the confident ones.

You're Not the Only One

Check the ones you've ever thought/ felt (be honest!):

- ⭕ "What if I leak at school?"
- ⭕ "I'm nervous to ask for a pad"
- ⭕ "I don't like changing in the locker room"
- ⭕ "I feel behind 'cause I haven't gotten my period yet"
- ⭕ "I feel weird talking about this with adults"
- ⭕ "I wish I felt more confident about my body"

This is your personal promise to treat yourself with kindness, always, especially on hard days.
Write your name and say it out loud, like you mean it!

I, _____, promise to:
- ✅ speak to myself with kindness
- ✅ allow myself to grow at my own pace
- ✅ remember that confidence takes practice
- ✅ be patient when I feel shy or unsure
- ✅ know that I am enough, exactly as I am

Sophie's Story #4
Embarrassed in the Locker Room

"Changing for gym class, I noticed a small stain on my shorts. My face turned red—I thought everyone was staring. But then a girl whispered, 'Hey, don't worry, it happens to all of us.' That moment changed everything. I wasn't embarrassed anymore. I felt part of a secret sisterhood."

Lesson:

Periods aren't shameful—they connect us.

4.3
What to Say If Someone Makes a Joke

Sometimes people — even friends — say things that make you feel small.
They might joke about periods, body changes, or even your emotions.
They might think they're being funny.
But you get to decide how it makes you feel — and how you want to respond.

Why People Make Jokes

-They don't understand
-They feel awkward
-They've heard others do it
-They're trying to be funny (but miss the mark)

Even if they don't mean to hurt your feelings, that doesn't mean you have to laugh along.

Here are a few calm and kind things you can say if someone makes a joke that makes you uncomfortable. Pick one or create your own!

"That's not funny to me."

"It's something normal — maybe you should learn more about it."

"Actually, it's just part of growing up. Not really a big deal."

"Would you say that if you had a sister going through it?"

"I don't joke about stuff that personal."

My own comeback idea:
_____
_____

Remember: you don't owe anyone a reaction.
Sometimes the most powerful response is walking away like a queen.

4.4
Body Confidence & Self-Love

Your body is changing — and that can feel weird.
But here's the thing: your body is not a problem to fix.
It's your home. It's strong. It's growing. It's yours.
And it deserves your love — even on the days you don't feel like it.

What Is Body Confidence?

It doesn't mean loving every single thing about yourself 24/7.
It means respecting your body, accepting its changes, and knowing it's worthy of kindness — no matter what.
Everyone has moments of doubt.
But learning to speak to yourself the way you'd speak to a best friend? That's the secret.

Things I Like About Me

Let's flip the focus. Write down three things you like about yourself — they can be physical, personal, silly, or deep. Anything counts!

_____

_____

_____

Body confidence isn't about being perfect.
It's about saying: "This is me. And that's more than enough."

4.5
Positive & Confidence Boosters

What you say to yourself matters.
Your thoughts can lift you up or drag you down — so let's make them kind, strong, and true.
That's where affirmations come in.

What's an Affirmation?

It's a short, powerful phrase that reminds you of who you are and who you're becoming.
You can say it in your head, whisper it in the mirror, or write it in your notebook. The more you repeat it, the more real it starts to feel.

Pick Your Power Phrase

Here are some ideas — choose one, or make your own!
- "I am strong, even on tough days."
- "My body is amazing and doing great things."
- "I am growing, learning, and becoming more me."
- "I don't need to be perfect to be proud of myself."

Create Your Mini Poster:
Turn your affirmation into something beautiful! Use this space to decorate it with colors, doodles, stickers, or shapes. Make it so you that you'll want to hang it up or tuck it into your pouch.

TRUE OR FALSE?

Mood Swings Mean You're "Too Emotional"

QUESTION:
If you cry one minute, laugh the next, and then feel annoyed five minutes later, it means you're being "too emotional."

True or False?

→ Answer at the bottom!

Sophie Says: Feelings don't make you weak — they make you human.

Answer: ✗ False! Mood swings are a normal part of puberty. Hormones can make feelings stronger and switch faster, but that doesn't mean you're "too much." It just means your body is adjusting

QUICK CHECK

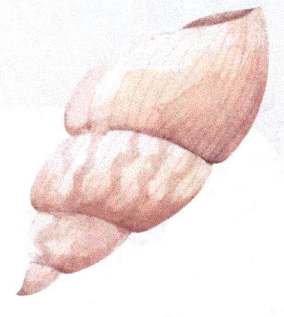

Which of these is the smartest way to handle an embarrassing period moment?

CIRCLE THE ANSWERS THAT ARE TRUE:

1. Panic and hide all day
2. Laugh it off or make a quick joke
3. Tie a hoodie around your waist and move on
4. Pretend it didn't happen and stay uncomfortable

✅ 2 and 3 are the smartest ways to handle it. ❌ 1 and 4 just make you feel worse. Everyone has awkward moments — they pass quickly!

PART 5
REAL TALK & PRO TIPS

5.1
Things No One Tells You (But Should)

There are some things about periods that don't get talked about enough.
Not because they're scary or gross — just because people forget to mention them!
But you deserve to know the real stuff. So here it is — no secrets, no shame.

Real Talk Truths

Your first period might be really light.
It could be a tiny spot of brown or red. You might even wonder if it's really your period — and that's normal!

Leaks happen. To everyone.
Even adults get caught off guard sometimes. That's why period kits exist. No shame. Just backup.

It might not be regular right away.
One month you get it, the next month... nothing.
Your body's still figuring it out.

You feel emotional or tired, even before it starts.
Crying at a movie? Craving pickles and peanut butter? Totally a thing.

Discharge is normal.
White or clear fluid in your underwear? That's your body getting ready. It doesn't mean something's wrong.

Cramps don't mean something is broken.
They can feel annoying, but they're just your uterus doing its job. There are ways to feel better — and you'll find what works for you.

You don't need to know everything right now.
You just need someone to tell you the truth — and remind you that you're doing great.
And that's what this chapter is for.

5.2
Periods at School, During Trips/ Sports

Having your period while you're out and about can feel like a lot.
I used to stress about it too, but once I learned a few tricks (and made a habit of planning ahead), I realized it wasn't as scary as it seemed. Here's how I handle it!

At School

Periods don't wait for after school. So keep a small pouch in your backpack with:
- ☐ Pads or liners
- ☐ Extra underwear
- ☐ Wipes or tissues
- ☐ Hand sanitizer
- ☐ A little note to yourself: *"You've got this, Sophie."*

💬 If you need help:
Ask to go to the bathroom or visit the school nurse.

On Trips or Sleepovers

Packing your period kit can give you peace of mind when you're away from home.
☐ Your favorite type of pad or product
☐ Pajamas you feel comfy in (just in case of leaks)
☐ A plastic bag (for used underwear or pad)
☐ A book, music, or journal
☐ Pain relief or heating patch (ask an adult!)

Bonus tip: Keep a long sweatshirt or hoodie handy — perfect for comfort and confidence.

During Sports or Gym Class

You can move, stretch, run, and even swim on your period.
☐ Use a product that feels secure (pad or tampon).
☐ Wear dark-colored leggings/shorts if you're worried about leaks.
☐ Let your coach or teacher know only if you need to take it easy — it's okay to rest.

Movement can actually help with cramps — so don't be afraid to keep doing what you love!

Sophie's Story #5
Period on a Trip

"My first period on a school trip felt like a disaster waiting to happen. I kept thinking, what if I leak on the bus? But I packed my survival kit, wore dark leggings, and told my best friend just in case. Everything went fine—and I even enjoyed the trip more because I knew I was prepared."

Lesson:

Preparation = peace of mind.
You've got this!

5.3
No Pad? No Problem!

Let's say your period shows up and you've got nothing with you. - No pad. No pouch. No backup.
First of all: don't panic. It happens. To everyone.
And there's always something you can do.

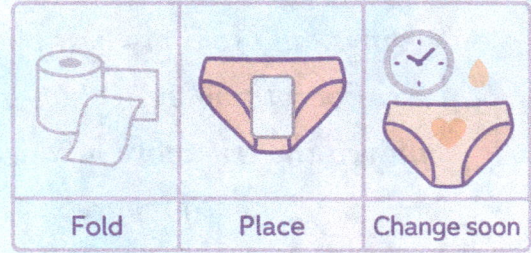

Fold · Place · Change soon

Here are some quick ways to handle the moment until you can get the real supplies:

1. Fold a few layers of toilet paper and place it in your underwear. Wrap it around the middle, and change it as soon as you can.
2. Paper towels or napkins: if you're not near a bathroom, folded napkin/clean tissue in your underwear can help.
3. Ask someone you trust. Most girls and women will totally understand — and be happy to help.
4. Visit the school nurse, front desk, or bathroom vending machine. Many schools and public bathrooms keep supplies available — you just have to ask!

5.4
What to Do in a Period Emergency

Sometimes, things don't go as planned.
Your period might start early.
You might leak through your clothes.
You might feel a sudden cramp that makes you want to curl up into a ball.
We call that a period emergency — and yes, it sounds dramatic, but the truth is: You've got this.
Let's make a plan so you always feel ready.

3-Step Emergency Plan

1. <u>Stay calm</u>. Take a deep breath. It's okay. You are not the 1º person this has happened to.
2. <u>Take action</u>. Get to a bathroom, use toilet paper as a temporary pad, change what you can, or tie a sweatshirt around your waist.
3. <u>Ask for help</u>. Find a trusted friend, teacher, or adult. Say, "I had a small leak, do you have anything I can use?"

SMART EXTRAS TO KEEP IN MIND

1. Leaks happen. Keep an extra pair of undies in your backpack.
2. Hoodies are heroes. Great for covering up.
3. Have a code word. Some girls have a fun phrase to say to friends ("Project Strawberry," anyone?).
4. Know where the nurse's office is.

My Personal Emergency Plan
Let's build your own go-to strategy! Fill it in below:

If I get my period at school, I will:

If I don't have a pad with me, I will:

If I leak and feel embarrassed, I will:

Someone I trust and could ask for help is:

**You are not helpless. You are prepared.
And with your plan in place, even an emergency…
won't feel so scary anymore.**

5.5
Myths to Bust

Let's face it: there's a lot of weird stuff people say about periods.
Some of it is just silly. Some of it is confusing.
And some of it? Straight-up wrong.
So let's bust those myths — once and for all.

You can't swim on your period. ✓ ✗
False! With the right product, you can swim just fine.

Everyone's period is exactly 28 days. ✓ ✗
False! Some cycles are shorter or longer: 21 or 35.

Period means you're "fully grown." ✓ ✗
False! Your body keeps growing after your 1ᵒ period.

You'd feel ashamed about your period. ✓ ✗
False! Periods are natural, normal, and something to never be embarrassed about.

You can't exercise during your period. ✓ ✗
False! Movement can help with cramps and boost your mood.

Periods are not dirty: they're a sign of health.

You don't have to hide your pad like it's a secret.

Boys should know about periods too: it's not a "girl problem".

There's no "right" age to start your period.

TRUE OR FALSE?

First Period at the Same Age

QUESTION:

All girls start their first period at the same age.

True or False?

→ Answer at the bottom!

Sophie Says: You're not "late" or "early" — you're right on time for you.

Answer: ✖ False! Some girls start at 9, others at 15 — both are normal. Your body has its own clock, and it's not a race.

QUICK CHECK

Which "Period Myths" Are Totally Made Up?

WHICH OF THESE ARE MYTHS (NOT TRUE AT ALL)?

1. You can't play sports on your period
2. Period blood is dirty
3. You can't get your period in the water
4. Chocolate cravings are always bad
5. Periods mean you're sick

✓ 1, 2, 3, and 5 are all myths
✗ 4 — cravings happen, and chocolate in moderation is fine.

5.6
Real Questions from Real Girls (Q&A)

You're not the only one wondering stuff.
So many girls have questions — even the ones who seem totally chill.
Let's answer some of the most common ones, just like a big sister would.

<u>"Will it hurt?"</u>
Usually, your period doesn't hurt — but you might feel cramps, like a sore belly or back ache. Annoying, but not scary.

<u>"What if I'm the last in my friend group to get it?"</u>
That's totally okay. Everyone's body has its own schedule. You're not behind — you're right on time for you.

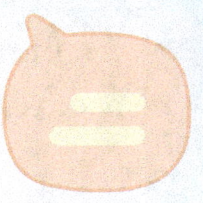

"What if I leak at school?"
First: breathe. Tie a sweater around your waist, go to the nurse, or ask a friend. Most people won't even notice.

"How do I tell my dad?"
Keep it simple: "Hey Dad, I got my period. Can you let Mom know?" You might even get a high five.

"What if I feel embarrassed just talking about it?"
That's normal. Start small — write it down, or tell someone safe. It gets easier the more you do it.

"What if I forget to bring a pad?"
Ask a friend, the nurse, or use toilet paper until you can get one. It happens to everyone.

"Do boys get periods too?"
Nope. But learning about them makes boys more respectful and understanding.

"Can people tell I'm on my period?"
Nope. Nobody can see or guess unless you tell them.

"What if I laugh and leak at the same time?"
It happens! Bathroom + hoodie around the waist = problem solved.

"Can I swim on my period?"
Yes! With a tampon or period swimwear, you can swim just fine.

"What if I drop a pad in the school bathroom?"
Pick it up, toss it, and move on. Every girl knows what it is — no big deal.

"What if I leak on the sheets at a sleepover?"
It happens a lot. Wrap things up, ask quietly for help — you're not the first.

"Can I still play sports?"
Absolutely. Movement can even help cramps.

"Why does my period sometimes look brown?"
That's just older blood leaving your body. Totally normal.

"What if my pad makes noise when I open it?"
Pads crinkle, but bathrooms are noisy places. Nobody's paying attention!

"Can I wear leggings on my period?"
Yes. Dark colors help if you're worried about leaks.

"Do periods ever sync with friends?"
Yep, it can happen if you spend a lot of time together. Science is still figuring out why!

"What if I feel emotional for no reason?"
Hormones can do that. Cry, laugh, hug a pillow — it passes.

"What if I forget what day my period will come?"
That's normal at first. Track it on paper or an app and soon you'll see a pattern.

"What if I feel embarrassed buying pads?"
Cashiers see pads every day. To them, it's just another item — nothing weird.

Got a Question of Your Own?

Here's a safe space to write it.
You don't have to show it to anyone, but you can if you want.
I've always wondered...

Sophie's Story #6
Talking to Dad

"I was so nervous to tell my dad I got my period. I thought he'd freak out or not understand. But when I finally blurted it out, he just said, 'Okay, let's make sure you have what you need,' and gave me a high five. I laughed so hard! Turns out dads can be way cooler than we expect."

Lesson:
Talking about periods doesn't have to be awkward—it can even be funny.

Appendix

When to Ask for Help

Hey, it's Sophie. 💖
Before we dive in, I want you to know something super important: most of the time, periods are totally normal. A little messy? Sure. A little confusing? Absolutely. But usually, nothing to worry about.

Still, sometimes your body might give you signs that it needs a little extra attention. And that's not a reason to panic — it just means it's time to ask for help from a parent, guardian, or doctor. Think of it like this: if your phone glitches, you don't throw it away — you check in with someone who can fix it. Same with your body.

This chapter is like a big sister's checklist of "red flag questions". I'm going to share the things girls often wonder about — the "Is this normal?" stuff — and give you clear, honest answers. Some answers will be: "Totally fine, no worries." Others will be: "It's smart to talk to an adult, just to be safe."

Remember, asking questions doesn't make you weak — it makes you strong. You're taking charge of your health, and that's something to be proud of.

What if my period lasts longer than 7 days?

I remember wondering the same thing. Most periods last 3–7 days, and that's totally normal. If yours sometimes goes a little over, it doesn't always mean something is wrong. But if it always lasts longer than a week, it's smart to talk to a parent and a doctor. They can check if your body just needs a little extra support.

💡 *Big Sister Tip: Write down how many days your period lasts each month. Having it on paper makes it easier to explain if you need to ask for help.*

What if my flow is super heavy (soaking a pad every 1–2 hours)?

I had a friend who felt like she was "flooding" through every pad — it stressed her out so much. Sometimes the flow is heavier in the first 1–2 days, and that's normal. But if you need to change your pad or tampon every 1–2 hours for several hours in a row, that's a sign to check in with a parent or doctor. You're not in trouble — it just means your body is working harder than usual and deserves some attention.

What if I haven't had my first period by age 15?

I remember worrying about being "the last one" in my group of friends. Some of them had their period at 11 or 12, and I kept waiting. The truth? Every body has its own clock. Most girls get their first period between ages 9 and 14. If you reach 15 and still haven't, it doesn't mean anything is wrong — but it is a good time to talk to a doctor, just to make sure everything's on track.

What if I get really strong cramps?

Cramps are common — I've had my fair share of lying on the couch with a heating pad and chocolate. But if the pain is so strong you can't go to school, sleep, or move comfortably, and simple tricks (heat, stretching, water, rest) don't help, that's a time to talk to an adult. Severe cramps can have different causes, and getting checked is the best way to find relief.

What if I faint, feel dizzy, or get a fever during my period?

Okay, this one is important. I once stood up too fast on a heavy-flow day and felt lightheaded — it scared me! A little dizziness can happen if you're tired or not drinking enough water. But if you faint, feel weak all the time, or have a fever with your period, tell an adult immediately. Those are signs your body might need medical help right away.

💡 *Sophie Says: Your safety comes first. Never ignore fainting or fever — it's always worth checking.*

What if I got my period but then it disappeared for more than 3 months?

When I first started, my cycle was all over the place. I skipped months, and it made me think I was broken. But that's normal in the beginning — your body is still figuring things out. If your period disappears for more than 3 months in a row, though, it's smart to tell a parent and see a doctor. It could be stress, sports, weight changes, or just your body adjusting. Still, checking in is the best way to feel safe.

What if I notice a really strong or unusual smell?

Periods have a natural smell — that's just part of the blood and discharge. But if it smells very strong, fishy, or unpleasant, that could mean an infection or something that needs attention. It doesn't mean you did anything wrong. Just let a parent or trusted adult know, so they can help ou get checked.

What if I see unusual colors?

Most of the time, period blood is red, brown, or even pinkish — and it can change from day to day. That's all normal. But if you ever notice gray, green, or unusual clumps that don't look like normal blood, it's a sign to tell an adult. Doctors are used to these questions and can figure out what's happening.

💡 *Big Sister Tip: Normal periods come in many shades — but when the color feels "off" to you, that's worth checking.*

What if I bleed in between my periods?

When you're first starting out, your cycle can be irregular — spotting in between are common. I had that too and thought, "Wait, am I starting again already?" But if the bleeding is heavy, happens often, or makes you worried, it's a good idea to talk to an adult. A doctor can check if it's just your cycle finding its rhythm or if something else is going on.

💡 *Big Sister Tip: Keep track of spotting in your journal — it helps you notice patterns.*

What if I have itching, burning, or pain down there?

I get it — even saying this out loud can feel awkward. But listen: itching, burning, or pain in your private area isn't something to ignore. Sometimes it's just from scented soaps, tight clothes, or not changing pads often enough. Other times, it could be an infection. Don't feel embarrassed — just tell a parent or guardian so you can get checked. Doctors deal with this all the time, and they know how to help.

What if I leak a lot, even when I change pads often?

Leaks happen — I've had them at school, at sleepovers, even at the park. But if you're leaking through pads or tampons even when you change often, your flow might be heavy enough that you should mention it to an adult. There are stronger products, like overnight pads or period underwear, and doctors can help too. You don't need to just put up with it

What if I feel super tired or weak every period?

I used to wonder if being extra tired during my period was "just me." Turns out, lots of girls feel drained. Some fatigue is normal, but if you're always weak, pale, or exhausted every cycle, it could mean your body is low on iron or losing more blood than usual. That's something a doctor should check. You deserve energy, not constant exhaustion.

💡 *Big Sister Tip: Pay attention to your body's signals — being tired all the time is not something you should ignore.*

What if I get headaches or migraines before my period?

I sometimes get headaches right before my period, and it used to confuse me. Hormones can actually trigger headaches or even migraines for some girls. A little rest, water, and turning off screens can help. But if the pain is very strong, happens every month, or makes it hard to do normal things, let a parent know. A doctor can suggest ways to make those headaches easier to handle.

💡 *Sophie Says: You don't have to "tough it out" — pain that interrupts your life deserves attention.*

What if I feel super sad or angry and can't control it?

Oh girl, I've been there — crying over a silly video one minute, snapping at my brother the next. Hormones can make emotions way stronger right before or during your period. That's normal. But if you feel really sad or angry a lot, or like you can't cope, talk to someone you trust. Sometimes it's just hormones, but sometimes your heart needs extra care too. Both are worth paying attention to.

What if I throw up or feel very sick during my period?

I once had cramps so strong they made me feel like throwing up — not fun at all. Mild nausea can happen, but if you actually vomit or feel very sick every period, that's a red flag. It could mean your body is struggling more than it should. Let an adult know right away, because you don't need to suffer like that. Doctors have ways to help.

What if I get cramps really strong?

Not all cramps stay in your belly — mine sometimes move into your lower back, and it feels like an annoying ache. Light stretching, a warm pad, or moving around can help. But if the pain is very strong and doesn't calm down, tell an adult. Severe pain anywhere during your period is a sign your body needs extra support.

💡 *Big Sister Tip: Your body shouldn't stop you from living your life. If pain keeps you from moving, it's time to ask for help.*

What if my cycle is very irregular (sometimes 20 days, sometimes 40)?

My first year of periods was totally unpredictable — sometimes two weeks apart, sometimes two months! That's common when you're just starting. But if your cycle is always very irregular, or suddenly changes a lot after being regular, it's worth checking in with a doctor. Stress, sports, or your body adjusting can all play a role.

💡 *Big Sister Tip: Track your cycles. Seeing the pattern on paper helps you know if it's really "irregular" or just part of the early stage.*

What if I have big clots (chunks of blood) in my flow?

The first time I noticed clots, I thought something was seriously wrong. But here's the truth: small clots (like the size of a raisin) can be normal, especially on heavy days. If the clots are really big, happen a lot, or make your period feel much heavier, it's a good idea to tell a parent and get checked. Doctors can help figure out why it's happening — and how to make things easier.

What if I can't do normal activities because of my period pain?

I've had days where I wanted to curl up and skip everything — but if pain keeps you from going to school, hanging out with friends, or doing what you love, that's a sign to get extra help. You don't have to suffer through it. Pain is your body's way of saying, "Please pay attention."

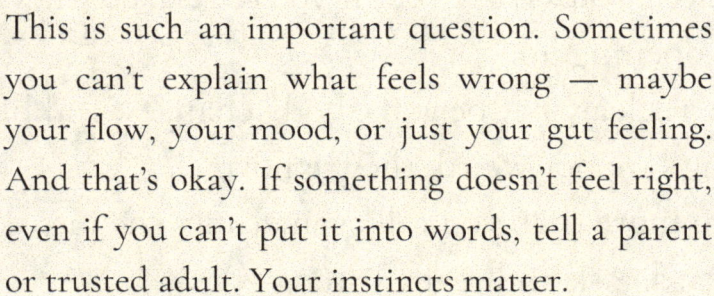

What if I just feel like something is "off" and I don't know why?

This is such an important question. Sometimes you can't explain what feels wrong — maybe your flow, your mood, or just your gut feeling. And that's okay. If something doesn't feel right, even if you can't put it into words, tell a parent or trusted adult. Your instincts matter.

💡 *Big Sister Tip: You don't need to have the "perfect words." Just saying, "I don't feel right," is enough to get the care you deserve.*

APPENDIX FOR PARENTS

Tips for Talking to Your Daughter About Puberty

Puberty can feel like a big milestone — for both your child and you. Whether your daughter is open and chatty or shy and unsure, these tips can help make the conversation feel natural.

1. Start small, start early: use everyday moments to introduce the topic without pressure.
2. Be calm and matter-of-fact: your child will take emotional cues from you. If you're relaxed, they'll feel safer opening up.
3. Make it clear that periods, body changes, and big feelings are not weird, they're normal.
4. Listen more than you talk: sometimes she just needs to be heard. Ask and really listen.
5. Keep the door open: let her know she can come to you any time — no question is silly, and no topic is off-limits.

A Sample "First Period" Conversation Script

Not sure how to begin? Try something like this:

Parent: "Hey, I found this book and thought it might help you feel ready when your period comes. I remember when I got mine — I had a lot of questions."

Child: "Yeah, I don't know much about it."

Parent: "That's totally okay! Everyone's body is different, and it's great that you're curious. You can ask me anything, or just read through this when you want. I'm here for you."

Tip: If you're not the primary female figure in her life, you can offer to connect her with someone she feels comfortable talking to — and still stay involved as a supportive presence.

Your Feedback Means the World!

I truly appreciate your feedback.

Thank you so much for taking a moment to share your thoughts! 🙏

www.ingramcontent.com/pod-product-compliance
Lightning Source LLC
Chambersburg PA
CBHW071902070526
44583CB00016B/1814